Original title:
Shifting Sands and Silent Waves

Copyright © 2025 Creative Arts Management OÜ
All rights reserved.

Author: Gabriel Kingsley
ISBN HARDBACK: 978-1-80587-383-9
ISBN PAPERBACK: 978-1-80587-853-7

## The Weight of Ocean Secrets

Bubbles rise, secrets dive,
Fish hold parties, can't survive.
Seaweed dances, gets quite bold,
Octopus juggles, tales untold.

Crabs wear hats, thinking they're kings,
Seagulls squawk, like they have wings.
A dolphin laughs, makes a splash,
But forgets his snack, what a crash!

## The Shape of Water's Whisper

Waves are giggling, rolling fast,
Splashing boats, a comical cast.
Turtles wear shades, think they're cool,
While starfish play, in their own school.

A clam's a lawyer, quite the catch,
Arguing shells, a salty match.
The tide pulls back, for a quick dance,
Mermaids joining, at a glance!

## Fleeting Impressions in the Mist

Fog rolls in like a sneaky cat,
Hiding crabs and the old hat.
Where did it go, that bright beach ball?
Oh look, there's a jelly, making a call!

Seagulls plot, to steal some fries,
Playing tricks, in goofy disguise.
As waves crash, the laughter flies,
With fishy gags, under gray skies.

## Discoveries Underneath the Surface

Down below in the ocean's home,
Fish play tag, in their own dome.
Treasure chests, full of junk,
Wait for divers, full of funk.

Coral castles, quite absurd,
Crickets chirp, oh wait, that's a bird!
Anemones tickle, with no shame,
As sea cucumbers join the game!

## **Mapping the Ocean's Heartstrings**

Bubbles pop like tiny jokes,
Fish wear hats and laugh in folks.
Crabs hold court on sandy thrones,
While starfish waltz with jelly tones.

Seashells gossip on the shore,
Whales burst out in songs galore.
Dolphins flip like fancier clowns,
And seaweed waves in silly gowns.

Turtles play in races slow,
But catch a wave, and off they go.
Coral reefs in vibrant hues,
Crack jokes with the tide's reviews.

In this world of aqua cheer,
Laughter rings from far and near.
Each splash and giggle, light and free,
Mapping joy beneath the sea.

# A Tale Woven by Currents

The tide's a clever little thief,
It steals your shoes, but brings you peace.
Nets of laughter, lines of fun,
Catch the rays, a golden run.

Octopus with crafty arms,
Paints the ocean with his charms.
Crabs do dances, quite absurd,
As seagulls squawk with every word.

A sea turtle's birthday cake,
Made of kelp and seaweed flake.
Blowfish puff with laughter loud,
While clownfish live, hilariously proud.

Underwater tales, bold and grand,
Woven tightly with a playful hand.
The laughter swells with every wave,
In ocean's embrace, we joyfully rave.

## The Dance of Shadows on Desert Shores

Beneath the sun, a dance begins,
With shadows prancing, where laughter spins.
A cactus winks with a prickly grin,
While seagulls debate where the snack is in.

The dunes do jiggle like jelly beans,
While camels check their fashionable scenes.
A tumbleweed rolls in with such flair,
Whispering secrets of who's unaware.

Sandcastles topple, the architects sigh,
As waves crash in with a mischievous cry.
The horizon winks, full of tricks up its sleeve,
Laughing at all who dare to believe.

## Transient Currents of the Forgotten Sea

Once there was a fish named Lou,
Who wore a hat that was bright and blue.
He swam with jokes that made crabs laugh,
While starfish practiced their very own gaffe.

Waves like giggles rolled on by,
Swirling tales of the gulls' sly lie.
A turtle joined in with a slow, grand move,
Grooving to beats only crabs approve.

Seashells chuckled at the scene they see,
Every barnacle grinning with glee.
The ocean sighed, 'Oh what a sight!'
Just wait for the moon to join the night.

## A Symphony of Grain and Grit

In a land where grains hold a surprise,
A drummer made of millet always tries.
With rocks as maracas, he keeps the beat,
While wheat grains shuffle by on tiny feet.

A baker once rapped, flour a cloud,
While butter crooned softly, feeling quite proud.
Jokes were baked in every loaf,
With giggles still fresh, they never are rough.

Mixers whirl like they're on the run,
Trying to dance, oh isn't it fun?
Sifting out laughter from overbaked bread,
With buttercream dreams and nutty thoughts fed.

**Serene Rhythms of the Horizon's Embrace**

The horizon stretched out wearing a smile,
Swaying to rhythms, oh what a style!
Clouds wear puffy coats, fluffy and bright,
Dancing in colors, oh what a sight!

The sun plays peek-a-boo, blazing but sweet,
While laughter bounces on the sun's warm heat.
A beach ball rolls by without any fuss,
Making friends with a surfboard, oh what a rush!

Seagulls topsy-turvy in aerial ballet,
As sandy footprints lead the way.
Each wave a giggle, every tide a joke,
In this vast stage, where silliness spoke.

## Epiphany at Water's Liminal Threshold

The ocean called, I wasn't keen,
In flip-flops stuck, my feet turned green.
A crab waved hello, with a sideways dance,
I pondered if it fancied a prance.

My sunscreen squirted, oh what a sight,
I slipped and slid, an unintended flight.
The seagulls cackled, what a ruckus they made,
While I clutched my towel, slightly dismayed.

## The Soft Murmur of Time's Flowing Veil

Time trickles down like sand through fingers,
As I try to recall all those songs that linger.
I hummed a tune, but the fish gave a stare,
"Is that all you got?" they seemed to declare.

My watch decided it needed a swim,
Splashing about, feeling rather dim.
With every wave that came to play,
My sense of time decided to stray.

## Beneath the Celestial Tide

A star fell down and landed in tea,
I chuckled, "Guess it's joining me!"
The moon winked twice, a cheeky soul,
As I tried to teach seagulls how to roll.

The tide pulled back, a grand retreat,
And I lost my flip-flop, oh, what a feat!
A dolphin laughed, or was it a jest?
I waved back, but found it too stressed.

## Vanishing Footprints on Salted Earth

I wrote my thoughts in the warm, wet sand,
But waves giggled loudly, "We have other plans!"
Just like my lunch, it was swept away,
Who knew seagulls liked burgers on display?

My footprints vanished like promised dreams,
As I chased a kite that burst at the seams.
With a whoosh and a zoom, it took to the sky,
And I stood there laughing, oh my, oh my!

## **Whispers of the Tidal Breeze**

The ocean's prankster plays at dusk,
Tickling toes with its salty musk.
Seagulls giggle, dive and soar,
While crabs do their jig on the sandy floor.

Waves toss hats like frisbees near,
Splashing laughter, having no fear.
A starfish waves back, quite a tease,
While jellyfish dance with all the ease.

Fish throw parties in coral masks,
As clams compete in old trivia tasks.
The sun dons shades, takes a recline,
As marine life breaks out the wine.

Underneath the tangled seaweed,
An octopus wonders, "What's your creed?"
But everyone's busy living the plans,
In this wacky world of ocean fans.

## Ephemeral Echoes on Dune's Edge

The dunes are bustling, a wacky sight,
With tumbleweeds sporting caps so bright.
A lizard zooms like a speedy car,
On a sandy stretch that feels bizarre.

Wind whispers secrets to each grain,
While the cacti laugh, poking in vain.
A rabbit hops with oversized shoes,
Claiming it's on the world's fastest cruise.

Footprints vanish as quick as a joke,
While the ghost crab dons a cloak of smoke.
A tumble down, it starts to sway,
And sand castles beg for a holiday.

Beneath the stars, the dance begins,
With twinkling lights where mischief spins.
In this realm of quirky delights,
Everyone's dancing through the nights.

## **Secrets Carried by the Gulf's Breath**

The breeze is a gossip, sharing the scoops,
As dolphins jump in outrageous hoops.
A pelican shouts, "What's the deal?"
While oysters hide in their shell conceal.

Crabs have a party with clam chowder dreams,
Spitting bubbles and marshmallow beams.
The shells all chuckle, a secret to keep,
While pearls giggle beneath the deep.

Tidal whispers tickle the shore,
As starfish gossip about the seafloor.
A quirky boat with a tutu sails,
While fish wear hats made of seaweed trails.

The moon joins in, wearing shades of blue,
And jellyfish float with a graceful hue.
Down on the beach, laughter prevails,
In this realm of bubbly tales.

## **Mirage Beneath the Moonlit Tide**


Under the moon, waves start to shout,
Calling the crabs for a mid-night rout.
Seashells practice their stand-up lines,
While the seaweed flops, forming strange signs.

Mermaids join in, with hair like foam,
Brushing sea turtles, making them moan.
A fish throws confetti, what a surprise,
As the starfish high-fives from the skies.

In the distance, a boat sings a tune,
Led by the laughter of the sleepy dune.
A nautilus plays the ukulele right,
In the glow of the silvery night.

Even the waves giggle and tease,
Riding the breeze like a summer breeze.
This watery realm under stars divine,
Invites us all to dance and align.

## **Melodies of Wind and Waxing Moon**

When the breeze plays tricks at night,
A kite flies up, oh what a sight!
The moon is grinning, round and bright,
While shadows dance in soft moonlight.

Sandcastles squabble, built too high,
A seagull swoops, it's said to pry!
The tide comes in, oh me, oh my,
And all our dreams just wave goodbye!

A crab in a tuxedo struts,
He tips his hat, he thinks he's nuts!
While waves compose a song, it cuts,
And leaves us laughing with full guts.

So if you hear the sea's sweet tune,
Join in the dance beneath the moon,
For nature's laughter ends too soon,
A giggle floats - our night's festoon.

## Secrets Held in the Tides of Time

A fish once told a tall, tall tale,
About a cat who wished to sail.
With jellybeans as his great trail,
He left behind a rubber whale.

The clock stands still upon the shore,
With whispers of the waves' soft roar.
Old crabs debate who's keeping score,
While dolphins dance and encore more.

A turtle tried to race a wave,
But ended up in a sea cave.
The tide sighed low, and then it gave,
To laughter that the sand will save.

Inside the sea, all secrets hide,
Like treasures lost on a bumpy ride.
With every ripple, they confide,
In moonlit laughter, they abide.

## Currents of Reflection on Moonlit Waters

Reflections twirl in playful spins,
Like fish who think they're wearing fins.
The moon, a judge with silly grins,
Watches as laughter surely wins.

Plenty of stars join in the fun,
While jellyfish light up, one by one.
A crab on stilts does a quick run,
Chasing the glare of the warm sun.

A log drifts by with a pirate's hat,
A fish swims up, says 'What's with that?'
Suddenly, we hear a splat,
As sea foam starts to do its chat.

With laughter echoing all around,
The night's sweet jokes become a sound.
In ripples, joy is always found,
The sea, a stage where fun is crowned.

## The Last Breath of the Leeward Shore

A sandpiper sings a goofy tune,
While pretending to be a raccoon.
The sun bows down, a golden boon,
And waves applaud the day's cartoon.

With each breeze, the grasses gossip,
While crabs plot mischief in their ship.
A clam, quite shy, lets out a quip,
Then skitters off with a silly flip.

The sunset's brush paints skies in glee,
As wave-kissed laughter floats with glee.
Each grain of sand joins in the spree,
Creating stories for you and me.

So let us cherish every joke,
That sea and shore, they surely woke.
In this great tale, we all invoke,
The humor shared — a gentle poke.

## Dreams Written on a Salty Breeze

The seagulls squawk, it's quite a show,
They steal your fries without a blow!
The ocean's laughter splashes high,
As jellyfish drift, oh my, oh my!

With every wave, a tale is spun,
Of mermaids lost and pesky fun.
A crab threw shade, that little brute,
I'd challenge him, but he's got no suit!

A lighthouse blinked, just like a star,
A beacon that guides lost folks from far.
But flashing lights might scare away,
The fish who thought they'd come to play!

So gather round, let's share a joke,
With salty squids and seaweed folk.
In dreams written on a breezy night,
We'll laugh 'til dawn, until the light!

## Melodies of Moonlit Wetlands

The frogs break dance upon the shore,
With all their hops, they beg for more!
A heron struts with swagger bold,
As twinkling stars watch from their fold.

Crickets chirp an offbeat tune,
While otters float and tease the moon.
They giggle, slip, then glide away,
A splash of joy at end of day!

The fireflies glow like disco lights,
In reeds that sway to easy sights.
They waltz around with all their might,
Making evenings feel just right!

The swamp's a party, loud and grand,
With friends that frolic, hand in hand.
In melodies of wetlands deep,
We'll dance and sing, then fall asleep!

## **Tidal Conversations**

The waves whispered secrets, oh so sly,
As fish swam by, just asking why.
A clam once grumbled, 'This is unfair!'
While barnacles chimed in with flair.

'What's this about tides?' asked a crab,
'Are they a friend, or just a nab?'
The starfish sighed, 'Let's just chill,
And ride the swells, it's quite a thrill!'

A dolphin joked, 'I've got a plan,
To learn to moonwalk like a fan!'
But with a splash, he slipped away,
Causing giggles in the bay.

As currents chat in whispered quirks,
A seagull laughs at all their perks.
In tidal talks, both loud and soft,
The ocean's humor drifts aloft!

## **A Journey Beyond the Shoreline**

Let's pack our snacks, it's time to roam,
To find the world beyond our home!
With buckets, spades, and hats so bright,
We'll chase the waves until it's night.

The sandcastles rise like towers tall,
But watch out, winds may make them fall!
A seagull swoops for a tasty treat,
While kiddos giggle in quick retreat.

Our footprints fade with every splash,
As surfboards glide in one big dash.
But who's that sinking in the wet?
A dad in shorts, we'll not forget!

With laughter echoing through the breeze,
We find our joy beneath the trees.
On journeys far from pure shoreline,
We'll make some memories, oh so fine!

## Lullabies of the Ocean's Caress

The crabs dance madly on the shore,
While seagulls squawk and beg for more.
Waves roll in with a playful shove,
Chasing beach balls, so full of love.

Sandy toes and sticky ice cream,
This beach is livin' the sweetest dream.
Umbrellas flop like wayward hats,
As coolers tip, spilling over spats.

A dolphin jumps, its flip a surprise,
Kids giggle, wide-eyed, in the skies.
Sunbathers snore, caught in a snooze,
While footprints erase the latest news.

The sunset glows, a disco ball,
As beach bums gather, one and all.
With laughter soft as the ocean's sway,
They dream of tomorrow, come what may.

## The Forgotten Path of Windswept Dreams

A tumbleweed rolls, oh what a sight,
Chasing its friends in a comical flight.
Dust bunnies giggle, twirling around,
As wind whispers secrets without a sound.

Kites take flight, in a slapstick dance,
Kids run away, giving fate a chance.
With ribbons tangled in hair and glee,
The air is a playground, wild and free.

Another gust sends hats flying high,
Parents chase after with a sigh.
The path is alive, in mischief it weaves,
Whistling old tales that the landscape leaves.

In the twilight, laughter lingers long,
Echoing softly, a joyful song.
The stars peek out, twinkling for fun,
As dreams swirl gently, one by one.

## Horizons of Memory and Mist

In the foggy morn, a pirate appears,
With a wooden leg and forgotten cheers.
His map is crumpled, oh what a joke,
A treasure hunt led by a silly bloke.

The sea calls out with a bubbling laugh,
As waves tickle toes, a watery path.
But shells conspire, whispering wise,
"Don't trust the seagulls; they steal the pies!"

Fog rolls in, like a giant's sneeze,
Mermaids giggle, hiding with ease.
Yet fishermen yawn, lost in their nets,
Counting their catch while making bets.

As shadows stretch, the mist starts to clear,
And all the ocean critters lend ear.
To tales of laughter, spun with a twist,
As memories bloom in the morning mist.

# A Tapestry Woven by Water and Wind

The river chuckles as it flows past,
Carrying tales from the present and last.
With frogs on lily pads, singing their tunes,
While dragonflies shimmer beneath the moons.

Old boats creak softly in laughter divine,
As fishermen argue over the best line.
The reeds wave like hands, cheering them on,
To catch the big one or just play along.

The clouds shift shapes, like hats in a shop,
Every gust brings a giggle or flop.
For each drop of rain wears a sparkle-pear'd face,
Dancing down to join in the race.

As dusk paints the tapestry, colors untold,
A masterpiece spun with mischief and bold.
Water and wind weave a world so tight,
With giggles and whispers, a comedic night.

## The Gentle Play of Light and Tide

Under the sun, the sea does grin,
With fishy jokes, it pulls us in.
Where gulls do dance and pirates joke,
Each wave a laugh, each splash a poke.

The crabs in suits, they run for miles,
Pretending to be suave with smiles.
While seashells whisper, secrets bare,
They giggle softly in salty air.

The boats all sway, a wobbly show,
As captains sway, the crew just glows.
With every breeze, a tickle here,
The ocean's jest, forever clear.

And when the tide takes off to play,
It leaves behind its frothy spray.
A canvas blank where laughter lands,
We paint our joy in shifting sands.

## **Ripples of Time Unfolding**

Time's a jester, poking fun,
With every tick, a little run.
Echoes bounce from wave to shore,
While seaweed waves, 'Just one more!'

The sand's a canvas for our toes,
Each footprint fades, as laughter grows.
Turtles giggle in their shells,
Sharing fables, ocean dwells.

The tide pulls back with teasing grace,
While jellyfish hide, a slippery chase.
The clocks dissolve, their hands unwind,
In this madcap realm, joy we find.

Each ripple tells a goofy tale,
Of clumsy fish and a giddy whale.
So let's forget the world so grand,
And dance with time upon the sand.

# Reflections of an Ocean Dream

In dreams, the sea is full of jest,
With dolphins donning each bright vest.
They jump through hoops of silver light,
While seagulls crack their corny bites.

The starfish laugh, stick out a limb,
As currents hum their cheeky hymn.
Each splashing wave, a punchline bold,
Where giggles echo, the night grows cold.

Crabs read fortunes in the muck,
Scheming plans, yet run amok.
The tide pulls in, with a wink and grin,
A game of hide-and-seek to win.

This whimsical world where nonsense flows,
Across the surface, the laughter grows.
Embrace the dream, let worries cease,
In ocean depths, we find our peace.

## The Soft Embrace of the Salted Air

The breeze whispers with a cheeky sigh,
As seagulls gossip about a pie.
The waves roll in and tease our feet,
While crabs and clams join for a treat.

"Look out!", the sandcastles cry and shout,
As little hands bring buckets out.
The tide giggles, splashes slow,
'You built it wrong, let's see you throw!'

The sun sets low, a painted sky,
While clowns in boats start passing by.
With fishy tales that tickle our ears,
We laugh aloud, despite our fears.

Embraced in salt, our hearts take flight,
Dancing together in the waning light.
So let's not fret if things go strange,
In this salty life, prove it's a change.

## **Time's Ebb and Flow**

The tide came in, my pants went out,
I splashed around, but oh, no doubt!
The fish all laughed, they swam with glee,
Said, "Why's he dancing? Is he free?"

To build a castle, I tried with flair,
But it collapsed like my summer hair.
Shells rolled away, took my dreams too,
I chased them down, like I could pursue!

A crab pinched me, I jumped and yelled,
In this beach drama, I was compelled.
With waves like humor, so wild and free,
Life's a stage, come laugh with me!

As shadows stretch, and sun bids adieu,
I gather my things, feeling quite askew.
Tomorrow awaits, with new tales to sow,
What goofy adventure will the tide bestow?

## Portrait of a Sea-Drifted Heart

I found a bottle, thought it was great,
Inside it was just a fish on a plate!
"Help!" it cried, "Need a better view,
Send me somewhere that's not with you!"

A dolphin winked, said, "Don't you fret,
At least it's a fish, and it's not a pet!"
We laughed and splashed, the sun aglow,
Still wondering where the ocean's flow goes.

A snorkeler sneezed, bubbles were flying,
As crabs did their dance, none were denying.
With every wave, my heart took flight,
In this comical drift, everything felt right.

So I sketch a life with colors so bright,
As clowns of the ocean play day and night.
With a brush and a dream, I dip and dare,
Creating a portrait, of laughter to share!

## Silent Reflections at Daybreak

The sun peeked out, what a sight to behold,
While I snorted my coffee, feeling quite bold.
Tides whispered secrets, I chuckled with glee,
"Shh! Not so loud, you're waking the sea!"

A seagull swooped, snatched my breakfast roll,
"Hey!" I shouted, "That's my crispy goal!"
With breakfast gone, my mood went down,
But the waves just giggled, never a frown.

As tides do their dance, the sea's got a plan,
They rolled on the shore like a nervous man.
Who knew reflections could bring such a laugh?
I'll let the waves chime in on my behalf!

So, as the day breaks with playful delight,
I wave at the sun, feeling quite right.
With laughter and joy, my heart starts to race,
In this joyful chase, let's pick up the pace!

## The Language Beneath the Waves


Bubbles speak softly, a gossipy crew,
Whispers of fish make the ocean feel new.
"Did you hear that? The current's a hoot,
Who knew the sea's gossip was such a flute?"

Shells hold our secrets, oh, what a chat,
They clip their shells like a capricious brat.
A clam just blurted, "What a fine day,
Tomorrow's forecast? More sun? Hooray!"

Starfish rolled their eyes, what a dull affair,
While octopuses juggled with casual flair.
They pulled a seaweed, did a twist and shout,
In this underwater ballet, joy's never in doubt!

So come take a dive, hear the tales they weave,
With laughter and bubbles, what a bright eve!
In the depths of the ocean, with echoes so grand,
Language flows freely, like laughter on sand!

## **Memories in the Grain**

A crab stole my flip-flop today,
He strutted along in such a weird way.
I yelled, 'That's mine!' with a laugh and a shout,
He winked and then scuttled all about.

Seagulls squawked like they owned the place,
I tried to reason, but it was a race.
They grabbed my sandwich, took off in a flash,
And left me with crumbs, oh what a clash!

The tide came in, my towel took flight,
Chasing it down felt so very right.
But the waves had a plan, they danced with glee,
My chase turned into a wet victory!

In the sand, my treasures got lost,
But laughter, you see, comes at no cost.
So here's to the grains where memories stay,
With a flip-flop thief, we laughed all day!

## Surrender to the Sea Breeze

The wind took my hat and tossed it away,
It spun in the air like it wanted to play.
I waved it goodbye, let it drift on the wind,
While sunscreen disaster was about to begin!

My buddy was buried, just peeking his head,
Digging him out was what he had dread.
His six-foot sandcastle, a fortress of dreams,
Looked like a lump, at least that's how it seems!

We splashed in the waves, our laughter a song,
But chocolate ice cream proved us all wrong.
It dripped on my shirt and stuck in my hair,
A sandy sweet mess that we both had to bear!

Yet through all the chaos and sandy delight,
We danced with the sea until the night.
With every giggle, we found joy with ease,
Life's a grand laugh in the sea breeze!

## Songs of What Lies Beneath

Diving for shells, what treasures I'd see,
But found an old boot instead, oh me, oh my!
Planned to grip pearls, what a fine little score,
Got a crusty old shoe, should I ask for more?

Fish in the waves giggled, making a fuss,
As I tried to sing out, could hardly discuss.
The fish rolled their eyes, swam swiftly away,
Perhaps they just didn't like my cabaret play!

Lost sunglasses mocked me from the tide,
They'd float on the waves, like they laughed, couldn't hide.
While seaweed wrapped round my leg in a dance,
I gave it a yank and laughed at my chance!

With all of this folly, who needs a crown?
A king of the beach, with my smile and frown.
So here we go, with a wink and a laugh,
The stage of the ocean is my favorite path!

# Fleeting Moments on the Dunes

We climbed up the dune, oh what a steep feat,
Only to slide down with laughter and treat.
Rolling in sand, it stuck to our skin,
A gritty surprise, where should we begin?

The sun beamed down, so we sought a cool shade,
But found instead a strange muscle parade.
The abs on display, oh what a sight,
They flexed and they grinned with all of their might!

I challenged one guy to a race by the shore,
He turned and he tripped; I laughed evermore.
The waves crashed and roared, it's a wet slip and slide,
With sand in our shoes, we twirled with pride!

As twilight approached, we gathered our gear,
Full of good stories and laughter to share.
For moments like these are treasures unplanned,
Life is a giggle, simple, and grand!

## **Shimmering Dreams upon the Water**

A fish wore a hat, how bizarre,
It danced on the waves, a true star.
With jellyfish friends playing a tune,
They rocked out together, under the moon.

The seagulls laughed, perched high in the sky,
As they watched the fish try to fly.
But they plopped back down with a splash,
And the waves giggled at the fantastic crash.

A crab joined in, clapping its claws,
Cheering the fish with a round of applause.
But when it tried to dance on its toes,
It slipped and fell, oh how it glows!

So they swirled and twirled with a wink,
These underwater jesters of ink.
In their shimmering realm, they found delight,
Living the dream beneath the moonlight.

## Portraits in Grit and Flow

A starfish tried painting, what a delight,
With colors of sunset, so vivid and bright.
It used its own arms, oh what a sight,
But confused a clam who thought it a fight.

The clam closed up, thinking bait was near,
While the starfish giggled, full of good cheer.
"I'm an artist!" it shouted with glee,
While all the fish gathered around just to see.

A shrimp came along, with a brush in its hand,
Said, "Do you need help, or is this all planned?"
The starfish just winked, shook its head side to side,
"Oh no, dear shrimp, I love this wild ride!"

So brighter and bolder, the colors did show,
In this gallery marine, where the wild currents flow.
Each splash and each laugh painted a tale,
In the humorous art of the ocean's wind gail.

## Shifting Colors of the Twilight Bay

At dusk, the crabs had a color fight,
Picking up paints, oh what a sight!
Red, blue, green, they splashed around,
A rainbow of chaos was soon to be found.

A turtle came by, with a frown then a grin,
"Don't throw that at me, I just polished my skin!"
But the crabs giggled, they were feeling so bold,
They painted the poor turtle bright pink and gold.

"Now I'm fabulous!" the turtle called out,
As the tide rolled in, shifting colors about.
With laughter like bubbles rising so high,
The whole bay erupted, like a comic reply.

So under the stars, they danced till the morn,
Crafting a spectacle, silly and worn.
In hues of the sunset, they'd laugh and play,
In the whimsical dance of the twilight bay.

## A Symphony of Shells and Sand

The shells once formed a band on the beach,
With a clam on drums and a conch that would screech.
They played with the waves, a musical flow,
Even the starfish would join for a show!

The sand tried to keep up, but oh what a mess,
Slipping and sliding, it couldn't impress.
So instead, it wiggled in sync with the beat,
A true sandy dancer, with no trace of defeat.

A blowfish popped up, puffed up with glee,
"I want to sing a note, bring it to me!"
But when it opened wide, the sound was quite strange,
The shells all fell silent, waiting for change.

The laughter erupted, a joyous decree,
As the sandy wind whispered, "Just let it be!"
So they jammed together till the sun came to rise,
In a concert of laughter beneath open skies.

## Twilight's Palette on Sun-Kissed Shores

The sun dips low, a cheeky smile,
Colors spill out, oh what a style!
Crabs doing salsa, they think they're slick,
While seagulls judge, with their beaks quite quick.

Beach balls flying, oh what a sight,
But caught in a net, they put up a fight!
Sandcastles tremble, they know what's next,
As waves come crashing, they feel quite vexed.

Flip-flops are flapping, a dance on the shore,
While sunscreen ninjas forget to rub more.
A picnic's a flop, with ants on the roam,
Their feast is a disaster, oh what a home!

But laughter rings out, a joyous call,
In twilight's glow, we embrace it all.
Life's silly moments, caught in a trance,
On sun-kissed shores, we'll always dance.

## The Embrace of Solitude and Surf

Alone with my thoughts, the waves share a grin,
They crash on the shore, where troubles begin.
A seagull swoops down, steals my last fry,
With feathers aflight, it's a sneaky guy.

Frolicking fish, a party of scales,
While starfish sit idle, and tell fishy tales.
Shells wear their makeup, a beauty parade,
While clams hide their shells, quite shyly displayed.

In the ebb and flow, I nod with delight,
As seaweed tickles my toes, quite a sight!
A breeze whispers secrets, it's all very bright,
Yet here comes a wave, giving quite a fright.

But solitude brews laughter, that sounds so grand,
Among surf and silliness, I take a stand.
A moment of bliss, in the ocean's embrace,
Where humor is found, in each splash and grace.

## Erosion of the Heart in Coastal Whispers

The ocean breathes softly, a sweet little tease,
Waves whisper secrets to crabs at ease.
A sand dollar dreams of becoming a star,
While dolphins giggle, amazing by far.

Hearts on the shorewrite their names in the wet,
But a rogue wave laughs, 'ah, not quite yet!'
With every retreat, love wears a grin,
As shells collect tales of where it's been.

Tides come and go, like a bad comedy show,
Where laughter erupts and sometimes it's low.
The gulls are the critics, with honks and with caws,
Reviewing the waves with their wings and their paws.

In this salty dance of life, we partake,
Where erosion is softening hearts with a quake.
So lift up your chin, let the humor abound,
For love in the waves is forever unbound.

## Silent Sentinels of the Breaching Wave

A wave rises high, like a jester at play,
Giggling and splashing, it steals the display.
Sea turtles trot by, with a wink and a nod,
As fish form a conga line, oh my, it's a squad!

The beach chairs are anchored, they flex and they sway,
Caught in a struggle with the sun's golden ray.
Picnic baskets tumble, decisive and bold,
While ants play the heist, their treasures unfold.

Yet look to the horizon, where humor resides,
In the dance of the ocean, where chaos abides.
Joy flows like water, full of life's whimsy,
With every breach, finds a chuckle so flimsy.

So gather your friends for a day of pure thrills,
As silent sentinels watch, caught in their chills.
The waves keep on breaching, promising mirth,
In the laughter of breezes, we find our true worth.

## The Emptiness Between the Waves

A crab danced sideways, what a sight,
Waving to gulls with all of its might!
Seagulls just laughed, said, "That's no grace,"
While a fish flipped over, splashing the place.

The sandcastle toppled without a care,
As kids ran for ice cream, joy in the air.
"What's happened?" cried one, with a frown so deep,
"The tide came to play, and it made a sweep!"

A beach ball flew, a dog caught the thrill,
Chasing it wildly up over the hill.
But it bounced off a head, much to their shock,
Now dog and man share a laugh on the block.

As sun begins to set, all is a giggle,
The waves take a break; oh, what a wiggle!
And crabs laugh at the drama that's passed,
In this silly game, nothing's too fast!

## Songs of the Sun-Kissed Shore

The sun sang low, with a twinkling tune,
As waves rolled in, on a bright afternoon.
Shells started clapping; a starfish would sway,
While puppies dove in for a splashy play!

A kid with a bucket, so proud of his catch,
Yelled, "Look, Mommy, it's a big ol' match!"
But all there was, was a hunk of wet sand,
Little did he know, a crab made its stand.

Towels flapped loudly as the breeze had a laugh,
A flip flop went flying, no way to turn back!
It hit the sunbather, who rolled on the sand,
Shouting, "Next time, just give me a hand!"

As shadows grew long, the beach came alive,
With seagulls and surfers, all ready to vibe.
Their silly shenanigans filled up the night,
As the waves sang along, what a glorious sight!

## Transition of Earth and Water

In one sunny spot where the water meets land,
The clams threw a party, it was quite a band.
They clamored for music and took to their feet,
But all they could find were shells, what a feat!

A turtle in shades grooved into the flow,
While otters played hopscotch, stealing the show.
The sand's not just dirt; it's a stage for fun,
Except for the crab who just wanted to run!

The waves whispered secrets to rocks on the shore,
Telling tales of the fish with dreams to explore.
"Let's ride the tide, see the world from afar!"
But they splashed quite a bit; it was quite bizarre!

As twilight approached, all creatures took pause,
Laughing at moments tossed out without cause.
The ocean chuckled and the land held their ground,
In this fruity buffet of hilarity crowned!

## Silence Between the Tides

Can you hear the sound of a flat, sleepy clam?
Snoring from dusk 'til the light turns to glam.
His buddy, the shrimp, said, "C'mon, let's bounce!"
But all he could do was shift, then re-prounce!

With each rolling wave, the whispers grew bold,
A sandpiper squawked, "Good grief, it's so cold!"
Shells gathered closely, exchanging a grin,
While a lonely old gull looked to dive and win.

It's a cycle of laughs, from sea to dry sand,
Watch out for the kid with the bright plastic hand!
He wobbled so fiercely, then took quite a dip,
Splashing all around with a comical flip!

When night fell asleep, and the stars twinkled bright,
Dancing reflections made the scene feel just right.
As the waves sighed softly, they too joined the fun,
In a lullaby laughter beneath the pale moon!

# Vestiges of a Forgotten Journey

While wandering through the dunes, I tripped,
A tumble like a tumbleweed, I slipped.
My map was lost, my snacks spilled too,
I laughed at footprints that led me askew.

Seagulls mocked, they flew overhead,
My hat flew off, I'd lost my head!
Chasing it down, I danced like a fool,
Turns out the seagulls attended my school.

A crab cheered me on, waving an arm,
Said, 'Hey buddy, you've got some charm!'
I offered a sandwich, he clutched it with glee,
On this wild jaunt, I made a new fee.

As sunset painted the sky a soft hue,
I stood on one leg, feeling brand new.
With a smile and a wave, the ocean said bye,
Next time, I'll remember not to fly high!

## Starlight and Seafoam

At night, under stars, I chased glowing waves,
Like a clown on a surfboard, full of braves.
I did a twist, a jump, a funny little dance,
The ocean just giggled, gave me a chance.

With each splash, the waves seemed to snicker,
I thought my midair pose was quite slicker.
But a rogue wave snatched my sandcastle dream,
Turning my fortress into a foamy scream.

The moon was my judge, shining so bright,
Laughed at my antics, saying, 'What a sight!'
I declared my defeat, but with lots of flair,
"Next time, I'll win! Just you, wait right there!"

With starlight as guidance, I wobbled away,
Promising the ocean, I'd learn how to sway.
A tidal wave bow, I took a deep breath,
Embracing the chaos, my funny friend's death.

## The Picture of Fluid Landscapes

A canvas of sea stretched wide as can be,
Where I painted my antics, a silly spree.
With a fine point of giggles, I mixed with the tide,
Creating landscapes where laughter's the guide.

My paddleboard wobbled like jelly on toast,
Every clumsy turn was a comedic boast.
As I carved out my path, I splashed and I slipped,
In this motion, my dignity lightly tipped.

A sand crab critiqued my artistic flair,
"How about some manners, or maybe a chair?"
I offered him seaweed, a wink and a grin,
"Let's collaborate, my crustacean kin!"

As the sunset draped gold on my splashy affair,
I turned to the waves, tossed my hands in the air.
With each liquid stroke, I declared a new law:
"Life's but a canvas, and I'm the goof's straw!"

## Messages Carried by the Wind

Whispers of breeze brought notes from afar,
"I've seen your dance moves, you're my favorite star!"
The leaves nodded softly, a giggly brigade,
Each gust packed humor, my worries betrayed.

With a paper boat hat, I took to the flow,
The ocean was busy, with jokes on the go.
A wave tossed my hat, gave it quite the spin,
Ha! Who knew water could also wear a grin?

"Take this message back," said a feathered friend,
"Tell the wind gales, I'm here for the blend."
I spread my arms wide, shouted back at the sky,
"Bring laughter and joy, let's all take a fly!"

As the wind whirls playfully, my spirit takes flight,
Chasing the whispers that glide through the night.
For every chuckle carried past shores of delight,
Nature's own humor brings smiles with its might.

## Transience Amidst the Coastal Mirage

A crab danced a jig, in the moonlight's gleam,
He tipped his hat, called it a team.
A seagull squawked, 'What's this fuss?'
The crab winked back, 'It's all just for us.'

The breeze blew soft with a playful tease,
A beach ball rolled by, coaxed by the seas.
A kid chased the ball, slipped on some goo,
Landed in laughter, 'I've joined the zoo!'

A picnic spread wide with sandwiches stacked,
When a hungry raccoon made a bold act.
He snatched a cupcake, with one little bite,
Then ran off giggling into the night.

The sun started setting, colors ablaze,
The ocean waved back in a spectacular phase.
A starfish exclaimed, 'What a curious mess!'
And the waves whispered softly, 'We love this finesse!'

## Reveries at the Edge of Existence

At dawn's early light, a dolphin did leap,
He shouted, 'Hey humans! Let's take a sweep!'
A beachgoer dropped his sandwich with haste,
Said, 'I came for fun, not for a taste!'

A star lay asleep, in the sand piled high,
Awoken by laughter, he let out a sigh.
'Can't you see? I'm a nap-sailing star!'
But the kids just giggled, 'You're still a bizarre!'

Along came the tide, with a tickle and splash,
Marked the shore's edge with a bubbly clash.
A conch shell exclaimed, 'What a graceful joke!'
As the seaweed danced with an elegant stroke.

And under the sun, things got odd quite fast,
A crab wore a hat, looking quite unsurpassed.
He strutted with flair, showed off his best side,
The waves just rolled on, in laughter they cried!

## Tides of Thought in Sandy Realms

A wise old clam sat snug in his shell,
Muttered to a fish, 'Is it just me or swell?'
'What is life's meaning?' asked the curious fry,
The clam shrugged and answered, 'Just aim for the sky!'

A tugboat chugged by, in search of a drink,
Colliding with seaweed, made quite the stink.
The dolphins all giggled, 'What a funny show!'
As the tugboat blushed, "I just wanted to glow!"

The horizon stretched wide, inviting the bold,
As a squirrel on the beach, made a home out of gold.
It gathered up treasures, shells in its pack,
While laughing at seagulls who'd try to attack.

Near a flickering flame, as sunset drew near,
Marshmallows roasted—it mingled with cheer.
A crab took a bite, bit into a toast,
Proclaimed with a grin, 'Sweets are what I love most!'

## The Lament of the Dune's Desires

A dune sighed softly, 'I yearn for some rain,'
'But every time I dream it, I wake up in pain.'
A butterfly fluttered, landed nearby,
Said, 'Don't fret, dear sand; just let the winds fly!'

The gulls made a ruckus, planning a heist,
'Grab those chips!' they chirped, 'We'll dine cold or diced!'
But the humans just laughed, and tossed them a snack,
Then slipped and fell over, sent their hat to the back.

A starry night beckoned with a glimmer of fun,
While the moon held a party, inviting the sun.
They danced with the waves, twinkling all around,
And a crab swooped in, in a polka dot gown.

With morning's first light, the ocean downplayed,
As the dune pondered how magic can fade.
It sighed once again, a life such a tease,
But couldn't stop chuckling, 'At least I have breeze!'

## **Echoes Beneath the Moonlight**

Under a sky that's slightly whacked,
The turtles dance, their shells all cracked.
Stars giggle softly, just out of sight,
While crabs throw a party till morning light.

Waves whisper secrets, they can't betray,
Seagulls join in, they know how to play.
With a splash and a slosh, they start to sing,
Who knew the beach was a comedic fling?

After a night filled with laughter and cheer,
The sandcastles tumble, oh dear, oh dear!
Fiddler crabs waltz, their little feet tap,
As the tide rolls in, they take a nap.

The moon gives a wink, "What a sight to see!"
It's a comedy show for you and for me.
So grab your popcorn, join in the fun,
The ocean's a stage, we're all number one!

## The Dance of Grain and Foam

A sand grain juggles, oh what a sight,
While bubbles do pirouettes, oh what delight!
The gulls are in costume, feathers all fluffed,
Doing the cha-cha, not one bit gruffed.

Tiny shells shuffle, they're feeling quite bold,
In this dance party, not one is too old.
The beach is a ballroom where laughter does reign,
Where mermaids laugh, and fish complain!

Coconuts dancing, rolling around,
While a clumsy starfish trips on the ground.
It's a waltz of grains and a jig of the foam,
The ocean's a place that feels just like home.

"Watch your step!" calls a clam with a grin,
As a wave rolls in, and the fun can begin.
But who cares if you fall? Just belly flop,
The tide will catch you, it's all a big hop!

## Unraveled Currents

A sneaky wave whispers, "Catch me if you can!"
But it splashes and giggles, a cheeky little plan.
Fish in the shallows are snickering too,
While dolphins are planning a comedic debut.

"Look at that human, splashing around!"
"Is that a dance or just falling down?"
With a flick of a tail, they laugh from afar,
As the tide rolls in, it's a wild beach bazaar!

Seashells lay scattered, like coins on the floor,
Each with a story, a laugh, or a roar.
The current plays tricks, it's quite a tease,
But the ocean wears humor like a summer breeze.

So grab your floatie, let's dive for a dash,
In the funniest waters, let's make a splash.
For life's just a ride on a rollercoaster wave,
With laughter and giggles, we're all quite brave!

## Secrets Beneath the Surface

Beneath the blue, where the sun loves to peek,
A luminous jellyfish gives a wink, oh so cheek!
While clowns of the sea, with their quirky attire,
Tumble and tumble, through ocean inspire.

Bubbles rise up, they tickle the sea,
And fish start to giggle, "Come play with me!"
A distant octopus plays hide and seek,
In rainbow-colored nooks, how utterly sleek!

Shells mutter secrets, they giggle and chime,
"Oh look at that diver, what a silly crime!"
Mermaids all snicker, their fins in a swirl,
Draped in seaweed, they've got style to unfurl.

With laughter and sprinkles, the sea's full of glee,
Where even the barnacles join in with a plea.
"Let's dance like the tides, let's leap with delight,
For under this water, everything's bright!"

## Serenade of Dunes and Distant Calls

A hermit crab wears quite a hat,
He struts around, thinking he's a brat.
The seagulls cackle, they won't relent,
Judging his style, it's time well-spent.

The dunes are dancing, oh what a sight,
They tumble down at the edge of night.
A tumbleweed rolls, oh where to go?
It waits for the breeze, just stealing the show.

A wayward sandcastle holds its ground,
Until a wave giggles, 'Come on, rebound!'
It waves in greeting, then hugs the shore,
Saying, 'I'll be back! Just wait and explore!'

In this wild place, humor never sleeps,
With sandy giggles and playful leaps.
Each grain of sand has a tale to tell,
Of laughter and folly, oh can you hear it swell?

## Beneath the Gaze of Celestial Waters

The stars above are quite a crew,
They make a wish, and then they brew.
A fish jumps high, thinking it's a star,
But splashes back, 'This isn't my par!'

The boats all giggle, swaying with glee,
They tease the waves, 'You can't catch me!'
While dolphins chat, sharing a joke,
As shells listen in, happy to poke.

A lighthouse beeps, 'I'm so bright, you see?'
The ocean replies, 'But you just flee!'
So they laugh together, from dusk till dawn,
Creating a song from dusk until gone.

With tides of humor gently rising,
Even the moon finds it surprising.
A dance so silly beneath the sky,
Where laughter echoes, oh my, oh my!

## Shadows on the Threshold of the Ocean

Footprints run in zigzag lines,
Looks like someone's had too many wines!
A crab scuttles, steals a glance,
Says, 'Hey there, want to join my dance?'

The shadows stretch, making shapes so wild,
Even the waves are a little riled.
A kite gets snagged, oh what a fuss,
Crying out, 'Did you bring a bus?'

A starfish challenges the waves to a race,
But the tide just giggles, picking up the pace.
They tumble and twirl, all in prank,
Sunsets grinning with a golden flank.

So join the silliness, let worries flee,
The coast is a playground, come dance with me!
Each shadow a story, a whimsical tale,
On this playful surface where laughter sets sail.

## Tangles of Tide and Time

Oh how the sea loves a good old prank,
She tosses old boats like they're just a plank.
The tide whispers secrets, then giggles away,
While clams argue who gets to sing the sway.

A tangle of seaweed, ain't it a mess?
It wraps around toes, causing distress.
But seaweed winks, 'I'm not that bad!'
While fish roll their eyes, they've gotten so mad.

Shells hold a conference, all in a row,
Comparing their colors, putting on shows.
The sun laughs brightly, lighting the scene,
With silliness reigning, oh what a dream!

Time may tick on, but who cares a dime?
With every wave crashing, there's reason to rhyme.
So let's join the frolic, and revel like fools,
In this world of wonders, where laughter rules!

# **Rhythm of the Eternal Shore**

On the beach, I lost my flip-flop,
Now it's dancing with the tide's hip-hop.
Seagulls squawk with a cheeky glee,
As I chase my shoe, oh woe is me!

The sunburned tourists all gather 'round,
While I do a waddle, what a sight I found!
Someone yells, 'Make a viral reel!'
But, with sandy feet, I just can't steal!

The waves crash in with a frothy cheer,
I scream, "Nobody told me to steer!"
A crab waves back, oh what a clown,
While I trip over shells, flopped flat on the ground!

With laughter woven in marine threads,
I fashion my crown from loose seaweeds.
At dusk, I'll brag about my day's spree,
A beach comber's tale, how wild and free!

## In the Embrace of Ocean Currents


Floating on a donut, soft and round,
I pretend to surf, but I'm stuck, oh bound!
Waves roll in with a gentle tease,
I grasp for balance, they laugh with ease.

A fish pops up, with a curious look,
"Is that your workout? You're off the hook!"
I splash back at him, he swims with a grin,
While I paddle madly, oh let's begin!

The sun blazes down as I take a dive,
But I'm greeted by sargassum, oh, I strive!
I'm a tangled mess in this green confound,
Giggling fish think I'm a water clown!

As evening falls, the tide pulls in,
I wave goodnight to my fishy kin.
Bobbling back home with jelly on toast,
I recite my tales, I'm the current's ghost!

# Traces Left by Wandering Feet

Footprints walk by, a zigzag race,
Did I really create such a comical trace?
The tide comes in, all my paths erased,
But oh, what fun in the water's embrace!

Shells chirp like crickets, an ocean choir,
I step on a jelly in a twist of mire!
With a shriek, I jump, it's a slip 'n slide,
As crabs cheer on from their sandy hide!

"Let's build a castle," a kid yells by,
I start a rampage, oh my, oh my!
Dumping sand like it's a magic feast,
I'm a sandy giant, from West to East!

At dusk we wave to the fading sun,
Counting the beach toys, it's all in fun.
Though my feet are bare and a little sore,
The traces I left are worth so much more!

## The Lullaby of the Distant Coast

The ocean hums a lullaby sweet,
While I waltz on waves, can't feel my feet.
A lifeguard whistles a snoozing tune,
And I'm pirouetting under the moon!

Tanned sunflowers dance on the sand,
With beach umbrellas, a colorful band.
I trip on my towel, the day's grand finale,
Making all viewers giggle, my own silly rally!

The sea foam giggles as it rolls and sways,
Tickling my toes in mischievous ways.
A clam gives a shout, "Hey, watch your step,"
But I trip, tumble, and start up the prep!

As stars wink down, I hit the straw,
Counting all my blunders while Madagascar's raw.
Swaying with dreams, in my sandy bed,
I drift off chuckling, with joy in my head!

## The Quiet Journey of Driftwood

A piece of wood with dreams so grand,
It floated by like a little band.
Waving hello to a fishy crew,
"Catch me if you can," said the branch that blew.

It saw a crab with a tiny hat,
Who scuttled away and thought, "How fat!"
In the shuffle and swirl, they made a dance,
The driftwood swayed, giving fate a chance.

Along came a seagull wearing shades,
"Don't mind me," it squawked, making the grades.
Driftwood chuckled, feeling quite spry,
"Who knew a coastline could be so fly?"

With a wave goodbye, it drifted on,
Beneath the stars, it sang its song.
"Life's a beach," it cheered with glee,
On this whimsical journey, wild and free.

## Beneath the Endless Horizon

A turtle lounged, oh what a sight,
With shades on its eyes, it basked in light.
"Why rush?" it said, with a wink of flair,
While sipping seaweed from a coconut chair.

A wave rolled in with a frothy laugh,
"Catch me if you can, I'm the bubbly half!"
The turtle just yawned, took a deep breath,
"Chill out, my friend; it's just ocean zest."

A crab came by, juggling some shells,
"I'm the circus star; hear the audience yells!"
With a flip and a twirl, it fell with grace,
The horizon giggled, "Now that's just ace!"

Together they laughed, under skies so blue,
In a world where silliness grew and grew.
"Life's meant for fun," the turtle declared,
With a surf of joy, its heart was bared.

## Reverie in Salt and Shadow

A jellyfish waltzed in the evening glow,
Checking its moves, putting on quite a show.
"It's all about rhythm," it said with flair,
"Who knew being gooey could give such a scare?"

A starfish chimed in with a clumsy spin,
"Let's dance together, let the fun begin!"
They shuffled and jiggled near coral bright,
Their laughter echoed into the night.

A clam looked on, just tapping its shell,
"Join our dance or hide in your cell!"
But the clam shook its head, "Too shy for that,"
As the jelly and starfish spun and sat.

But soon curiosity won, it joined the song,
With pearls of laughter where all belonged.
In the salt and shadow, they spun a tale,
Of friendship and giggles that would never pale.

## When Tides Recede

Oh, when the ocean pulls back its robe,
Seashells peek out, like a fashion probe.
Starfish on duty, holding their pose,
"Look at us shine, in this sandy nose!"

A sand dollar giggled, "I'm rich, you see!
Got wishes galore; come and wish with me!"
But a curious crab snapped, "Aren't you so bold?
In this little world, the treasures unfold!"

A seagull perched high, surveying its land,
"Who needs a plan when you've got grains of sand?"
With a flap and a flap, it tried to be cool,
But bellyflopped hard into the ocean pool.

Under waves that chuckled, the tides returned,
The treasures all danced; their spirits burned.
With salty puns and laughter so wide,
They floated away, on the outgoing tide.

## Footprints Fading in the Light

Footprints dance on the beach,
Leaving tales of each step.
Seagulls laugh overhead,
While crabs hide in a pep.

A jellyfish floats by me,
With a wobbly sort of flair.
I tripped on my own laughter,
And now I'm stuck in the air.

Waves tease my sporty hat,
As they frolic and splash.
I swear it had a good run,
But now it's a fishy trash.

The sun giggles at my tan,
As I flip-flop through the spray.
I'm a mermaid in my dreams,
But a sunburned fool in the day.

## Storylines Written in Grit

Granules pile up high,
Each one a story told.
A wind tells secrets softly,
While I sip my lemonade cold.

Kites fly into a kite fight,
As laughter fills the air.
Like soap bubbles, our plans pop,
And disappear without a care.

In this sandy saga, I write,
With a shovel as my pen.
Each stroke a joke or a prank,
That changes now and again.

A sandcastle stands proud,
With a moat forged from fun.
But a wave of conversation,
Makes it melt, oh what a run!

## Horizons that Call Us Home

The horizon does wobbly dance,
Winking like a cheeky friend.
I chase clouds in flip-flops,
Where the sky and sea blend.

With every splash, I giggle,
As sand flies in my face.
The sun is now our DJ,
Spinning tunes for our race.

Here come the beach ball soldiers,
Bouncing into the fray.
Like unexpected ninjas,
They make the dull fade away.

As waves whisper my secrets,
I can't help but burst into song.
My adventures are so silly,
I can't believe they last this long!

## Patterns Linger in the Night

Under the moon's quirky glow,
Shapes twist and swirl with delight.
Shadows play peek-a-boo games,
While I dodge with all my might.

Footprints shift like a cat's pounce,
Tracing silly designs anew.
In the grainy wonderland,
I'm both the artist and the zoo.

Stars wink, join the mischief,
As I attempt to take flight.
With each giggle from the cosmos,
My dreams scatter in the night.

We dance like grains of sand,
Mixed with stardust's silly fate.
In this playground of shadows,
Where laughter and fun await.

## Carried Away by the Current

A crab in a hat, what a sight to see,
Dancing on pebbles with glee in the sea.
Fish gossiping softly, on gossip they thrive,
While a seagull nearby swoops down to arrive.

Surfboards in tow, they race like mad,
Dude, where's my towel? This is getting bad!
Flip-flops are flying, and laughter's a wave,
As sand gets everywhere, oh what a grave!

Seashells collect tales of slip and of fall,
Mermaids have parties, but don't invite Paul.
A whale with a wig is DJing tonight,
Underneath shooting stars—what a glorious sight!

So carry your cooler, your snacks and your chair,
Splashing with joy without a single care.
Just watch for the tide pulling all things away,
Especially that sandwich you left out to play!

## The Lure of the Half-Moon Shore

When the moon's on the rise, the sand starts to giggle,
As crabs tap dance, and fish start to wiggle.
Laughter erupts from the beach's wild crew,
While seagulls attempt their best stand-up too.

A sunburned fellow forgot his sunblock,
Turns out his beach towel is quite the hard rock.
He rolls like a sausage, red as can be,
Crab-cheering ensues! Oh, what a sight! Whee!

Starfish congregate for their nightly debate,
Discussing the wonders of their droppy fate.
A lone sea turtle yells, "It's existential!"
But the tide rolls in fast—this is purely accidental!

As laughter resounds from the foam-laden sky,
The waves pull you in, it's hard not to fly.
So dance with the tide and let whimsy take hold,
At the half-moon shore, you're never too old!

## Untold Stories Written in the Sand

Footprints in patterns like spoodles on sand,
Leaving behind stories they never had planned.
A seahorse doodling, some driftwood's a pen,
Tales of lost snacks and a beach ball's great zen.

A flip-flopper struggles, oh what a big mess,
While seeking the treasure that didn't impress.
"Is this a gold coin?" he asks with a grin,
But it turns out it's just a bottle cap din.

The waves come in close, like friends at the door,
Whispering secrets that they can't ignore.
Bubbles are chuckling, the tide starts to sigh,
Writing down lives on the sand till they die.

So gather your memories, bake them in sun,
Share giggles and stories, oh isn't it fun?
All fade by evening, as darkness begins,
Yet laughter lingers, where the sea forever spins!

**An Odyssey Wrapped in Foam**

In a land of great bubbles, where dolphins wear ties,
A whale started rapping—much to our surprise!
With a beat from the ocean, he grooved with finesse,
Mollusks bobbed along—oh, what a hot mess!

A parade of sea sponges, swaying with flair,
Clam shells were cheering, a quirky affair.
They juggled jellyfish, surprising the crowd,
While starfish tried limbo—oh yes, that was loud!

Flicks of fish tails splashed all around,
As bath toys conferred on adventures they found.
A lost rubber duck quacked, feeling quite bold,
"Let's sail back to childhood, stories retold!"

So slip on your flip-flops and join in the cheer,
In a frothy adventure where fun's always near.
The ocean's a canvas, where laughter's the norm,
Creating an odyssey, all wrapped in foam!

www.ingramcontent.com/pod-product-compliance
Lightning Source LLC
Chambersburg PA
CBHW062112280426
43661CB00086B/493